A collection of Paul's Poems
(Volume three)

Paul Scrivener

For Sylvia

Paul

This book is dedicated to Vicky Bodo and Nigel Washington without whose help and guidance these poems would never have been published.

First published in Great Britain by
Sitting Duck Press
2 The Avenue
Flitwick
Bedfordshire MK45 1BP

ISBN 978-0-9575823-3-0
A catalogue for this book is available from the British Library

Book & Cover Design: Sitting Duck [www.sitting-duck.org.uk]
Printed in the UK by Imprint Digital

Contents

Foreword

It is an honour to commend this volume of poetry to you. Copies of Paul Scrivener's first two anthologies have been well received, and deservedly so. With a relaxed approachable style and a selection of topics which stir the reader, Paul has creatively engaged with his public and produced two helpings of rich delight. And now we have more!!

So what is different in this volume? Well, not a lot really. Why change what is so successful? The poet is possibly in a more care free mood, very confident in his brief, but in essence we have familiar topics and similar themes: nature, England, a bygone age, the whimsical way with things, the meaning in life and love of place(s). All these are delivered with a wonderful, natural, day to day style, sometimes simple but never simplistic, often nostalgic but rarely sentimental, evocative and sometimes revelatory, occasionally clichéd but never corny, sometimes bravely original but always joyful as if written in a twinkle of an eye.

Paul Scrivener, with his musing and amusing, unpacks life and gives us an autobiographical airing of sights and scenes, with reflections that are simultaneously splendid and special. He captures the local Norfolk diction with wit and affection and descriptions of places like 'stubby, scruby Breckland' are to be applauded. 'Symphony of Seasons' is masterful and when stirred by the sea our poet is in his element, 'beneath those water, O so calm, a waiting danger lurks.'

An indeed the air is 'soggy with nostalgia' especially when the pen is turned to cars, comics, ciggies, corner shops and buses of every regional colour. This is marvellous reverent revisiting of the past where the reader can happily revel.

Then there is the humour. At frequent turns we have wry lines, puns and sparkling wit. There's 'A Marriage of Convenience' for Mrs Armitage Shanks, would you believe and Mr Dunne, the salesman is 'done in a turn', and the PC Santa is 'lost and totally helpless, all because of political correctness'. These are just a few of the characters you'll meet in this volume. You may even recognise yourself at some point.

Just as we are fully seduced into Paul's safe, gentle and finely observed world he strikes us to the core with some piercing, poignant moments and lessons for life. 'Force Ten to Safe Harbour' is paradoxically harrowing and comforting. 'Undying Love' is deeply moving and 'Memorium at Wells' is quite noble and graphic, social history observed.

Volume Three, 'Sunset, is an honest outpouring of a goodly soul, so if these poems are really to be Paul's last offering I suggest that you read them very soon. Find a quiet corner and a comfortable seat and with your favourite drink by your side, arm yourself with this anthology and drift into another world in the company of a poet who is both a friend and companion for the journey.

Revd. Nigel Washington

May 2014

General

Arras 1917

Three men from three regiments fought there,
Three men from three regiments died,
They did not know each other
For the battlefield was very wide.

Ernest's with the third battalion
Of the Bedfordshire Regiment,
Aged twenty he sets his sights on the goal
Then charges, both brave and defiant.

Charles is with the Essex'
From a village of just eighty souls,
The officers give the orders
And the young lad does as he's told.

Albert is a sergeant with the eighth Bedfordshires
And is senior to all of his men,
The order is given, "Come on", he cries
And is never to be seen again.

Somewhere in all of that wasteland,
A cemetery now has grown,
And among the many thousands,
Three men have an 'unknown' stone.

Fast forward to the twenty-first century,
There's no near relative to care,
But I, in my ancestry tracing,
Have found this burden to share.

You see, Charles was my mother's cousin,
Ernest my uncle would have been,
Albert was my grandfather,
These men I had never seen.

So this year on eleventh November,
I have a good reason to stand,
And remember people now with names
Who were once the flower of our land.

Buttons

Buttons white and buttons black
Buttons brass for jackets slack
Buttons large and buttons small
Buttons used by one and all
Buttons with pictures transferred on
Pink for daughter, blue for son
Buttons small for shirts and blouses
Big ones used to mend men's trousers
Odd ones cut from worn out 'cardis'
(Ones we've dumped 'cos they've got tardy)
Buttons new for us to use
Buttons old give us the blues
I know someone you won't outfox
'cos they're all in Granny's button box.

Caroline

'Caroline' appeared through the lichen on the stone,
Who was she? What was she? Where was her home?
Was there a husband? What children did she bear?
Did anyone ever stop and put a nosegay there?

The stone was one of many laying in that place,
Did people lying there die in God's good grace?
Was her life so precious that she had a granite stone,
And at the end did she decide for sin she should atone?

In quiet solitude they lay, generations from the past,
Sitting on an old oak bench I wondered who'd been
    the last.
Some have flowers planted in their little garden space,
But most had wild flowers, growing there apace.

The churchyard was neglected for few now worship there.
It seems as if this generation really cannot care.
But I wondered what she did, or was, and then, where
    was her home,
This lady who was Caroline and named upon the stone?

Deraliction

For years people passed by the little house
Now all ivy-clad and quiet as a mouse,
Boarded up windows, the garden a mess,
Unoccupied for thirty years plus.

Who had lived in this faraway cot',
Elderly parents? Children not caring a jot?
Were children born there – now living close by?
Do they pass the old cottage and give a sigh?

What stories an old house can tell us,
Of Christmases, birthdays, happiness, fuss.
Was mother house proud? Did they have running water?
Did parents raise children, a son and a daughter?

The ivy now seeks to invade the inside,
A main road is built so it nestles beside,
The shrubs which were planted have grown so tall,
Their leaves smother the garden when they start to fall.

Now house, you still stand there, a sorrowful sight.
Will nobody buy you and put you to rights?
Paint peeling, slates missing, family all gone,
Your story has ended and nature has won.

Ding Dong

I spotted it in a lay-by,
One hot summers day.
I checked what was in my pocket
For I knew I would have to pay.

I approached it very cautiously,
Unsure what to say.
I'd seen it their occasionally,
But on no specific day.

Suddenly a noise came forth,
Very loud and out of tune,
It told me that someone was there
Although it was early June.

My courage was very important,
All fears now had flown,
I went up to the thing and said,
"I'd like an ice cream cone".

Going with a Bang

Driving through towns and villages
On a bleak November day,
You will notice various adverts
For a firework display.

Village 'A' has a show of note
According to the poster,
A "MAMMOTH" display is there for all,
Rockets will roller coaster.

Village 'B' can go one better,
A "GIGANTIC" display is there,
Bonfire and Barbecue attracts
You'll need your winter wear.

Village 'C' is not out done,
Their display is "HUGE",
A band and funfair is promised,
(And dancers from Moulin Rouge?)

No matter how they're advertised,
Whether in east or west,
The one that will surely always win
Is the one just called "THE BEST".

Heroes

The surgeon said, "I will operate,
Your toe I will put right,
But you will have to rest it up
Or you won't feel very bright".

At first I felt aggrieved, then pleased,
I'd be able to walk again.
It would only take a week or two
Then I'd be as "right as rain".

We often think just of ourselves
How selfish we are at times,
Just watch a programme of war-torn lands
And limbs blown off by mines.

The fighting forces, men and girls,
Put their lives on hold,
Trying to stop insurgents
With skills both great and bold.

Those folk will never be the same
Although given help to cope.
What they have lost can't be replaced,
A future full of hope.

When we really stop to think
About our aches and pains,
They are so insignificant
As we have much more to gain.

Holiday '46

What a year in '46 when holiday time was here!
The clothes were all packed into a trunk and labeled
    very clear,
Collected by the railway man to be delivered Saturday
To the seaside boarding house where we had booked
    to stay.

We only had the clothes we wore the rest had all 'gone on',
New clothes and ration books went where the sun
    just shone.
Train tickets were duly purchased and departure times
    were checked,
The first holiday since before the war, it surely can't
    be wrecked,

But they'd not reckoned with their son, a lad of only eight,
One look at him on Friday night and they realised
    their fate,
A mass of spots was on his face and on his body too,
Chicken pox was what he'd got, whatever should they do?

There was no food left in the house, ration books
    had gone,
No phones to let people know what had happened to
    their son.
The holiday of course was lost, a burden they had to bare,
I don't know how they managed – 'cos I was too ill to care.

Holidays by the Sea

Just a week or to ago this harbour park was full,
The summer visitors were here for coastal holidays have
  a pull,
But now the summer's waning and the nights are pulling in
Those happy holidaymakers have gone away again.

It's such a brief season to make the most of the sun
And seaside traders have stocked their shops hoping
  visitors will come,
The British weather is so fickle, it's not always hot
But Britishers are used to it and do not mind – a lot.

The seaside remains in situ no matter what the season,
And people love to live there for whatever reason,
But what of those who visited, perhaps travelled
  many miles,
Did they go home happy with brown faces wreathed
  in smiles.

The housewife spoke of resting, the husband told his
  chum
Of the wonderful old ale houses and the things that they
  had done,
But the children when they returned, to face their school
  once more,
Had to write about it in an essay which really was a bore.

Hooked Up

Have you ever wondered how an engine pulls a train?
The carriages just roll along as the loco takes the strain,
Stand upon the platform and watch the ganger man
As he hooks up the engine by a well used working plan.

The loco, a mighty hundred tons, created by mankind,
The ganger man (or fireman) stand on the rails behind,
A chain hangs from the loco, heat and brake pipes too,
To attach them to the carriages he knows what he must do.

The loco gradually backs until the buffers almost touch,
The heavy chain is lifted and placed on the carriage hook,
Safely it is locked in place, then the pipe is raised,
If the loco's near enough the driver will be praised.

I really can't imagine a much more dangerous job,
Than to stand upon the rails and hear the loco throb.

Indications

There's a bridge across a railway in a little market town,
A roundabout on either side causes motorists to frown,
It seems most are able to negotiate one (with a fuss)
But to drive around the second one, well, you'd think they
    drove a 'bus.

The Highway Code says keep to right if second turn
    you'll take,
But which is first or second ? - so amnesia they fake.
If a driver's not too sure, then he just keeps in the middle,
Then he simply adds a vacant look and with the rear view
    mirror fiddles.

There is a gadget in the car which is mostly never used,
It lights up little arrows if right or left you choose,
But this is far too awkward for our little motorist friend
So he simply holds his breath and goes swinging round
    the bend.

Now, maybe it is just my view when I see these
    people drive,
They seem to have no sense at all, I don't know how
    they thrive;
Do they never have a plan in life, don't they know which
    way to go?
Don't they realise it's right to indicate in the traffic flow?
It must be sad for those he knows as he meanders on
    life's way,
Maybe he'd find directions if he'd only stop and pray.

Ironing

You have to have the iron hot
But sometimes only warm,
Often you have to steam the clothes
Of various shapes and forms.

A pile is made for cottons
And one for poly mix,
Silk is in another one,
If they're wrong you're in a fix.

Why can't the clever boffins
Make an iron which can tell
The difference between materials
And adjust itself as well.

To make it much more homely
A pretty cover's on the board,
Of course, you cannot see it,
It's covered with clothes, an iron and cord.

Now, how do you iron fitted sheets
With corners of wretched elastic?
Make sure in shirt pockets there are no cards
'cos you cannot iron plastic.

All this ironing is very boring
I wish somebody would now call,
For if I drifted off to sleep
Then from this stool I'd fall.

L. S. Lowry

To call the work of Lowry
His "little matchstick men"
Is a travesty in the art world,
An insult beyond our ken.

Look beyond the predominant figures,
People are there by the score,
But in the background are the buildings,
Painted as never before.

The dark satanic mills are there,
Depicted without fear,
Waiting to despatch their goods
To boats at Salford pier.

Lowry's work is not all bland,
He's painted men at play,
The football stadium he knew
Was alive on Saturday.

So now we understand his view
How he saw the scene,
And maybe considered wistfully
How it might have been.

But warehouses and stadia
Are dead and must come to life,
So people going to and fro
Came from his pallet knife.

People going about their work,
Upright, or backs bent,
To show it as it really is
Is Lowry's art intent.

Mithered

Why is it when you get up late
Everything goes wrong?
You go to buy your newspaper
And your favourite one has gone.

You arrive home hot and bothered,
Have your morning cough,
Then fill your bowl with cornflakes
To find the milk's gone off.

Never mind, you'll have some toast
The grill lights with a splutter,
The toast is done when alarm bells ring,
You forgot to buy some butter.

And so you boil the kettle
To make a cup of coffee,
You'll have it black, you take the jar,
It's damp like brittle toffee.

The car is giving trouble
So you remove the coil
But then you notice, with surprise,
Your shirts got covered in oil.

The day just goes on and on and on
When will your problems end?
You pour out all your troubles
When you bump into a friend.

It seems his day is just like yours,
Maybe even worse,
All you can do is laugh it off
(Or have a little curse).

So you agree to go together
To a restaurant out of town,
Naturally when you get there
You find the place pulled down.

One Hundred Years On

They died, those young and gallant lads,
For what? A future they never had?
Whose war was it? Was there a reason?,
Did the enemy attack first? Was the cause treason?

Governments in their ivory towers
Talk and manipulate for hours and hours,
They then sign treaties to help one another
Which often makes brother fight against brother.

Because of agreements signed long ago
Families face hardship, destruction and woe,
Ordinary decent folk living in peace
Find themselves hated as hostilities increase.

These lads were brainwashed to fight for the right,
Whose right? Not theirs, just a government indite,
No 'adventure' was this, for as such it was sold,
And they marched to disaster and conditions untold.

Millions of men are remembered by name
Listed on marble, with proper acclaim,
One hundred years on we stand, heads bowed bare,
And wonder what governments sent them there.

Premier League Cricket
(Bedfordshire)

Well now, that's a rum un',
In county cricket league,
You don't expect no errors like
Or 'memory fatigue'.

Last week the opposing team
Were getting out right quick,
And batsman number ten got out
With first ball – very slick.

Number eleven, he weren't ready
So rushed to get pads and hat,
He was so very mithered
He forgot to take out his bat.

It didn't make much difference
He were out the very first ball,
Not that he saw it coming
Until he heard the umpire's call.

They were all out for ninety-four
So then it was our turn,
Slasher Jimpson had first hit,
To win was his concern.

The ball sailed up into the air
Over the sight screen high,
And landed with a graceful 'plop'
In the river flowing by.

They tried to reach the cricket ball,
With a long handled fishing net,
And ribald jokes from spectators
Made the best entertainment yet.

Cont.

The umpires fetched another ball
So the game could begin again,
Slasher gave that a mighty whack,
The umpires looked in pain.

Over the other sight screen
The ball sailed Oh so free,
And to the birds annoyance
It landed in a tree.

Slasher promised to behave himself
As ball number four was used,
The opposition, who had lost the game
Went home quite bemused.

Premier League Cricket
(Norfolk)

There's a seaside town in Norfolk
With a lovely cricket ground,
The team itself is not too bad
Makes others jealous I'll be bound.

It once was very open
With trees, not overlooked,
But developers soon found it
And were well and truly hooked.

A doctors surgery was 'needed',
Very useful in the town,
So on a sunny summer day
Half the trees came down.

The ground then looked lopsided,
"Lets build on the other side",
So two nice blocks of flats were built
And removed the trees which hide.

The ground is still quite central
With buildings all around,
Which means the teams have nowhere to park
Within half a mile of the ground.

Now, Norfolk lads will not be beat,
They're full of tricks you know,
So when a ball is bowled at them
It gets a mighty blow.

Cont.

Sometimes it runs to boundary,
Sometimes it's in a mix,
But when Whacker Johnson gets a go
He hits a mighty six.

Up in the air the ball will sail
Soaring like a plane,
Until it gets up to the flats
And goes through a window pane.

"Cor blast it bor," he's known to say,
A stroking of his hair,
"I allus hit the ball that way,
How long hev thet bin there?".

Somewhere Else!

"What was that you were saying, my dear?
I must be getting quite deaf"
(In actual fact I was miles away
Having watched Masterchef).

It was the same when I was at school,
The teachers would go rabbiting on,
What was happening outside the windows
Seemed to be much better fun.

As a child I was expected to go
To Sunday School also to Church,
I tried to listen and understand
But concentration was left in the lurch.

Business meetings were necessary but dull,
An intelligent expression was great,
But if I had ever been rumbled
That would surely have sealed my fate.

It is such a joy to go travelling
And very much cheaper too,
If you can perfect day-dreaming,
By waking up right on cue.

The Lady with the Smile

Many times I passed her door,
Who she was I did not know,
But beside the track a bank was there
Where many flowers grow.

It was always such a pleasure
To pass the flowers fair,
For beside those riotous blooms
The lady was always there.

Driving past or walking
There was a smile and a friendly wave,
So it did not matter how 'down' you were
Much joy to you it gave.

Now it is so different,
True, flowers still bloom there,
But due to her infirmity
The lady is not there.

She gazes wistfully from inside
As people still pass by
Looking to the future
With moisture in her eye.

Twitching

Whatever are they doing
Out there in wind and rain,
Anoraks and 'Barbours'
It just seems so insane.

They stand there in their wellies,
Their faces in a grin,
Water dripping from their hats
And soaked through to the skin.

Telescopes are pointing,
Binoculars are raised,
What is it they have spotted,
Can they see it through the haze?

A little brown bird singing,
Or the one from Berkeley Square?
What ever they are watching
I bet it knows they're there.

Everyone has hobbies,
Most can be called 'sane',
But what type of person
Likes standing in the rain.

There'll be a letter in the "Telegraph",
"The Times" will have one too,
All because a little bird
Flew in out the blue.

Typical!

It was very hot today
Too hot to go about,
Last week it was far too cold
I would not venture out.

As usual I went shopping,
(I always do on Friday)
But only found half what I wanted
That shop's gone past its heyday.

Then, of course, the car won't start
It has become a pain,
And when I go to fix it
That's right! - it starts to rain.

The train was due at two o'clock
I went early for my ticket,
There I found a great long queue
It really wasn't cricket.

Why do planes fly over low
And make an awful noise?
It's almost as bad at the school gate
With crowds of noisy boys.

Nothing seems the same today
It's not like I've always known,
Yet, the world would seem a poorer place
If I couldn't have a moan.

Whether Wise?

Wherever do they get them from
These folk who look so bright,
They tell you what the weather will do
But seldom get it right.

The little man we love to hate
Got it half right – again,
"Tomorrow it will be warm and dry"
It poured down with warm rain.

This morning, for example,
The sky was cloudless blue,
But according to the lady
There'll be gales all day through.

And have you noticed on the face,
A look of exaltation
When they are able to forecast
"There'll be precipitation".

A foot of snow, you may recall,
Was forecast for last week,
Not quite right (again), we got
Ten minutes worth of sleet.

Of course there is a good excuse,
"We can't be that specific,
It's coming from the Atlantic,
(Or maybe the Pacific)".

There's just one forecaster who's right,
It's very plain to see.
He knows exactly how it is,
That forecaster is me.

Who's There?

The train pulled into the station,
A young lady alighted that day,
She obviously was a stranger
Looking for somewhere to stay?

She stood outside looking lost
No bus or taxi was there,
She showed the porter a paper,
An address which on it did bear.

You'll have to walk all the way
And it's a two mile walk I'm afraid,
But the pathway is very straightforward
You need get there before the light fades.

Eventually she found the right road
Then the address which she sought.
There was no reply to her knocking
So she opened the door, feeling taut.

Somewhat bemused she look round,
It was not a room that she knew,
The furniture and curtains were very old
But from the window there was a good view.

She suddenly heard people talking
And there began a feeling of dread,
But she gently pushed the door open,
"Are you my grandma?" she said.

Wholesale Happiness

What makes people happy
For happiness is free,
I've joined this happy band
And I'm as happy as can be.

Happiness is for everyone
Imagine a happy world,
Where politicians banter happily
And a happy flag's unfurled.

How a sandbag can be happy*
Takes happiness too far,
I'd be much more happy
To see a happy morning star.

A holiday in Happy Valley
Would make happiness complete,
You would go home feeling happy
With happy dancing feet.

Happy is go lucky
And happiness all around,
When we happily go together
To that happy hunting ground.

*"Happy as a sandbag" is a musical play.

You Can Please Some of the People

...

Two ladies entered the restaurant,
The younger one was eager to please,
But the older one (her mother) was different,
She was giving out looks that would freeze.

They were shown to a table by the window
Where the sea could be easily seen,
Said mother, "I can't see very much
The window could do with a clean".

She spoke (not quite!!) in a whisper,
The daughter looked harassed to death,
"It's a carvery dear, look at that meat",
Which was met with an intake of breath.

"You can have as much as you like dear,
They know you're an octogenarian."
"I'm not eating meat", her mother replied,
"Since breakfast I'm vegetarian".

Natural England

Ashridge at Christmas

Christmas time is one of stress
Buy extra food, maybe a new dress,
The Day itself goes by in a blur,
An enjoyable time we will all concur.

Next day we need to stop awhile,
Go for a walk, climb that stile,
Drive over and walk through Ashridge wood,
See and listen to all that is good.

Families meet up and have a chat,
Talk about Christmas and this and that,
Walk down paths, leaves crunch underfoot,
Down by the pingo we spy a coot.

Sitting quietly on a seat we spy
A small herd of deer passing by,
The daylight fades, we must go home
While nature the woodland floor will roam.

The next time that we will come this way
There'll be a bluebell carpet, a glorious display.

A Symphony of the Seasons

Good composers write a symphony of four distinctive parts,
They start with spirit as if to say 'we are in such good heart',
The second movement is much slower, it's getting
    second wind,
Third and fourth raise up the tempo and complete it in
    a spin.

And so it is with nature, that too comes in four parts,
The first part is the springtime, a good way for years to start,
The summer is much slower as we laze in sunshine haze,
The autumn breezes and winter chill bring hard and
    powerful days.

SPRINGTIME is an opening, a waking time for all,
Flowers start to open and birds begin to call,
The world seems very fresh to us, a new life now begins,
A cacophony of sounds are heard and nature's in a spin.

In the fields young life is seen as lambs new born are found,
There are splashes in the rivers as drakes chase ducks
    around,
Birds have started nesting and bees seek out the flowers,
We will start to live again in daylight's longer hours.

The SUMMER is always welcome with long days and
    sunny times,
A time for all to slow down and the world is in its prime,
Trees in leaf and lambs are growing, baby birds have
    fledged,
Gardens ablaze with colour, flowers glowing in the hedge.

Cont.

People go on holiday, abroad or perhaps at home,
The beaches will be crowded, you'll never be alone,
If your taste is not the seaside then set out for a farm,
The animals are safe in fields so there's no need for alarm.

Come AUTUMN the fields are barren except where sugar
    beet is grown,
Fields which were harvested have once again been sown,
Mud is spread by tractors going from field to field,
And the countryside's no longer tidy, more like a
    battlefield.

The trees are loosing all their leaves as autumn chill arrives
Beech nuts and horse chestnuts help small animals survive,
Leaves turn brown and flutter down, the wind blows them
    about,
And the feeling in the air has changed, of that there is no
    doubt.

The hardest time for us to face is when WINTER comes
    around,
We know there will be frost and snow which hardens up
    the ground,
At Christmas time we don't much mind and like to see
    some snow,
But on the first of January we wish that it would go.

The birds will find it difficult and rely on us for food,
Nuts and fat balls all hung out make them, and us, feel good,
Beneath the surface of the ground bulbs prepare to flower,
First snowdrops then the crocus and we're back in
springtime's bower.

And so the symphony has ended, the baton is laid down,
But the world will keep revolving in village and in town,
The tides will ebb and flow again, we live by God's good
    reasons
For we will always live within the symphony of the seasons.

Breckland

Stubby, scrubby Breckland
Straddling Norfolk and Suffolk Counties,
The best of country 'hot spots'
To find out nature's bounties.

Stubby, scrubby Breckland
Is were rabbits still abound,
Watched over by the warreners
Food for mediaeval towns.

Stubby, scrubby Breckland
You'll find Thetford forest there
So you can walk or cycle
And catch Red Squirrels unaware.

Stubby, scrubby Breckland
Looks nothing driving through,
But in Swaffam and Castle Acre
There's plenty you can do.

Stubby, scrubby Breckland
Has two thousand varied plants,
Bilberry, Heather and Storksbill,
Common Cow-wheat and Corn Cant.

Stubby, scrubby Breckland
Has buildings by the score,
Oxburgh Hall and Gooderstone,
Cockley Cley and many more.

When you visit Breckland
You'll find history and nature there,
Wildlife and activities
Are there in equal share.

Day or Night

Some folk reckon on getting up early to face the
  coming day
Pulling back the curtains and , maybe for a moment, they
  will stop to pray,
They listen to the old cock crow and watch the birds
  wake up
Then hasten to the kitchen to find the tea-bag and
  the cup.

It's true that early morning air has not been breathed
  before
And the clear blue sky and birdsong thrills us to the core,
We're well prepared to sally forth and start our daily
  round
For there's no better time of day that will be ever found.

Mind you, we do not all think the same and prefer the end
  of day,
We look out at our gardens where moonbeams start
  to play,
The daily toil is ended and we can now relax
And change into tee-shirts, jeans and perhaps a pair of
  slacks.

So which of these do you prefer, daytime or the night,
Cockerels crowing to wake you up or owls in silent flight?
It does not really matter, there is no wrong or right,
What matters most is what we do between morning time
and night.

Deep Blue Sea

How do we view the deep blue sea on summer days?
Children paddling at the edge, sand castles which amaze,
But beneath those waters O so calm a waiting
    danger lurks,
The deadly currents wait to strike, on 'Neptune's' face –
    a smirk.

Because we are an island race we're governed by the sea,
When a north-easterly force ten blows it's not for you
    and me,
But fisherfolk and merchant men seek harbour for
    their safety,
Whilst communities who live close by watch as the sea
    gets angry.

Their pagers call the lifeboats out, a yacht did not take
    heed,
It's now capsized, to save the crew a lifeboat is what they
    need,
So drenched, and sorry for themselves, they're brought
    back safe to land,
The lifeboat crew don't want rewards – just pleased to
    give a hand.

Rip tides and North Sea surges will make seafarers care,
And if you cross the Morecambe Sands, a guide will take
    you there,
Dogger, Thames and Humber, Finistaire and German Bight,
The weather forecast in an area will surely keep you right.

Never take a risk at sea whether surf-board or a sail,
As, it matters not the weather, summer sun or gale,
The deep blue sea is dangerous, precautions you must
    take,
Take notice of the notices or you could seal your fate.

Face the Weather

It's always been a puzzle
But now I know the reason why
The seagulls always face the wind
And look up to the sky.

They look so very comical
A great flock in awful weather,
They face the wind so that it does not
Ruffle up their feathers.

Of course, they know a thing or two
And learned to face the trouble.
Whilst folk just turn their backs on it
And live life in a bubble.

Fruitfulness

Driving along a country lane
The hedges looked unkempt,
For this was early Autumn
And summertime was spent.

There were no longer flowers
And yet it all seemed well,
For there were many blackberries
Hips and hoars as well.

Some bushes were festooned
With fluffy 'Old Man's Beard',
Crab apple trees had ripened fruit
But late night frosts were feared.

And so the year is put to bed
Then the world can spring anew
After its rest that comes in winter
The snowdrops will spring to view.

Garden Joy

Gardening is not a chore, in fact, it's very pleasant,
You work among the birds and bees and, maybe, the
   odd pheasant,
It makes you very happy, relaxes and brings smiles,
And if the garden's large enough you walk for miles
   and miles.

Of course, there can be problems, disappointments and
   some fear,
The times the mower will not start for the first cut of the
   year,
Seeds which grew two years ago no longer germinate,
And cabbages have pretty leaves just like grannies lace.

Grass seed, newly set, has gone, the pigeons think
   it's theirs
And when the hosepipe has a kink you'd better say your
   prayers,
You walk back to turn the tap (so the water can't get
   through)
When the build up disconnects the lot and the water jet
   hits you.

Why do carrots go all bent instead of being straight?
Cyclamen keel over when for weeks they've all looked
   great,
The leaves on the geraniums look like Emmental cheese,
And there's no flowers to be seen, so there are not any
   bees.

We can always blame the weather (and the government
    takes a hit),
But, hang on just a minute – have we always done our bit?
Maybe the mower should be serviced before winter
    storms begin,
And seeds that did not germinate should be kept dark in
    a tin.

Set new seed and cover it because the birds don't know,
They just want to eat it before it starts to grow,
Grow carrots in fine soil if you want them to be straight,
Pick bugs off the cabbages if you want veggies on the
    plate.

The moral is quite simple, its a bit like living life,
God will give a helping hand, it's us that causes strife,
Gardening, like life, can be disaster or be bright
If WE grow in the way we should by doing all things right.

Home County

England has many counties
Going from East to West
North and South and in between
There's one I love the best.

It has no sandy coastline,
It's easy to overlook,
But for all its many failings
It's lovely in my book.

Yes! It is commercialised
There's three industrial towns,
But there's the Chiltern Hills escarpment
Known as Dunstable Downs.

It has a zoo of great renown
Thousands visit it each year,
There's also a well know brewery
Which, people say, brings cheer.

The County town of Bedford
Has many open spaces,
And on the flowing River Ouse
There's often rowing races.

The Northern part is rural
With many a village street,
A duck pond and a Parish Church,
A hall where people meet.

Bedfordshire has everything
Which a 'native' can desire,
And when I come back home again
It sets my heart on fire.

Just Fishing

The gulls flock round the harbour mouth
In the air or on the sea,
Little gull and Herring gull
(They look alike to me).

With piercing cry they wait for boats
They know when they'll arrive,
The fleet have been out fishing
And for morsels the birds will dive.

Distracted somewhat by the crowds
Who throw them scraps of food,
The garrulous flock are tempted
For they spy something good.

Not all are old hands at it,
The young ones are not sure,
They look around bewildered
 And speculate in awe.

Soon the fishing boats are seen,
Expectations now run high,
The birds all rise up as one
And darken out the sky.

They make themselves a nuisance
As the boats unload the catch,
The gulls are quick, the men are quicker
As they batten down the hatch.

Marching On

A whirligig of weather, that is March,
Winter clings to the last vestiges of sleet,
Spring edges in, trying to evade notice
And somewhere in the middle they are bound to meet.

It is not possible to predict what will come,
We must anticipate that daffodils will follow crocus,
Yet the chill wind blasts us back indoors
Our stinging eyes, still running, cannot focus.

But wait and watch, nature is not fickle,
Truly seasons change, surreptitiously they creep,
We may not notice, but nature is aware,
And lambs are gambolling within a flock of sheep.

So do not doubt what seasons bring along,
They will always appear to us to be a haze,
We must accept what Mother Nature sends,
And with grateful hearts sing out a song of praise.

No Need?

The river flows at a steady pace
Wonderfully environmental,
The 'gin clear' water goes along
There's no need for a lifeboat on the Ivel.

People walk on the river bank,
The pathway has approval,
It's safe to walk all pathways there
There's no need for a lifeboat on the Ivel.

The river flows past Jordans Mill
An updated working revival,
It's open to the public – so
There's no need for a lifeboat on the Ivel.

It's amazing what you find there,
People's rubbish will bedevil,
And injure all the wildlife – still
There's no need for a lifeboat on the Ivel.

And so there is no need to fear,
Agree the lifebelts removal,
After all, it's just a stream
There's no need for a lifeboat on the Ivel.

... BUT ...

Someone has just fallen in
It's urgent for survival,
He's trapped in weeds and current strong
We NEED a lifeboat on the Ivel.

The river's overflowed its banks
Although it's nothing coastal,
People are flooded in their homes,
Send a lifeboat up the Ivel.

Our Lane

It looks just like an ord'nary road,
Common to those who use it,
They go up and down most every day
And there's a seat where they can sit.

The road's been there for many a year
It was first a winding lane,
So many bends, it slows cars down,
Safely cycle just the same.

Stop and look across the field
There's barley and there's wheat,
And those funny parsnip looking things –
That's lovely sugar beet.

The banks, (if they're not all cut back),
Are full of colourful flowers
Which prettify your journey
From March to winter's showers.

Then, of course, you hear the birds,
Robin, thrush and rook,
Maybe a cuckoo in the spring
Or nightingale to book.

Hedges grow on either side,
They reckon you can tell
How long that has been growing there
By the variety in which there dwell.

Within the hedgerows stand some trees,
Sycamore, oak and ash,
Some of them are long since dead
Wearing ivy like a sash.

Cont.

Some things vary with the seasons
But folk are always meeting,
As people travel up and down
They give a friendly greeting.

The road goes through the village
Past the pub, the Church and brook,
A road that folk use every day,
Why don't they stop and look?

Our Village Fete

Roll up, roll up, enjoy yourselves,
There's stalls where you can buy
And if you're really lucky
For a sideshow prize you'll try
At our village fete.

Your garden should look pretty
But there's a corner where
A plant bought at the plant stall
Will make the garden fair
At our village fete.

There's a bookstall with many hundreds
Of authors old and new,
Go and have a good old browse
And buy up one or two
At our village fete.

You will never need go hungry
There's plenty here to eat,
And of course a cup of tea
Always goes down a treat
At our village fete.

If it's animals you're after
There is no need to fear,
For you'll find a unique white elephant
(That's a stall of course) that's here
At our village fete

Cont.

The church today is glowing
But needs funds to revive,
There's plenty needed to be done
To help it to survive,
So everything you spend today
Whether pennies or in pounds,
Will save for generations
This church and lovely grounds
In our village.

Summer Nights

How lovely are those balmy evenings
When sitting on the village green,
Watching a lively cricket match
Between two rival village teams.

Swallows darting overhead
Catching insects in the air,
We sit there watching on wooden bench
And only the players have a care.

It's quiet now the day is done
Apart from some mighty 'thwacks'
As willow hits leather for the umpteenth time
And fielders attempt to take the catch.

The match at last is over,
The sun turns the sky dark red,
And players go off to their home
Dreaming what might have been, asleep in bed.

The Gate ...

It stands alone, sentinel to the field,
The wood, once sturdy, to time and weather yields,
For forty years it's seen the seasons change,
Spring to summer, autumn, winters weather range.

Memories of equipment through the gate won't fade,
From men with scythes to combine's multi-blades,
Open when it is needed but shut tight to keep folk out
Yet rabbits, pheasants, hares, just go between the bars,
  the closure flout.

... To the Field

Inside the field crops will grow apace,
Rotation yearly equal to arable space,
One year maybe sugar beet will be planted row on row,
The next year machines move in and start barley seed
  to sow.

Sun and rain, cold and warmth help the crops to grow,
Green shoots are seen, then watch the barley glow,
Soon the crops are ready and the big machines move in,
The tranquillity is shattered by the combines roaring din.

Every field has its gateway, some wooden, some of steel,
A gateway to the crops which mankind grows with zeal.
A lifetime of experience is the field that we sow,
But the gateway must be open for those experiences
  to grow.

Up There

There's always something new to see up there,
Just look, you will not see the same sky twice,
Except, may be, on summer days when it is clear,
Not like today with puddles spiked with ice.

The sky was grey, but now we see the sun,
It's partly covered by a long thin cloud,
Yet its very edges are brightly lit as one...
Great illumination, golden glory, shouting loud.

Now watch carefully, you'll see what's coming next,
A crowd of little ones, water boys, in a row,
Yet that feels to be right out of context,
Maybe it will fall with just a hint of snow.

Look! Look! It's changed again and lost its gold,
It's turning pink with clouds sharp, blue, precise,
Daily, hour by hour, the heavens change unfolds,
Just look, you will not see the same sky twice.

Village Centre

Every village has a centre where folk love to meet,
It could be in a building or even in the street,
There's a place to have a mardle as it has for generations
It's there we put the world to rights, it helps to save
    the nation.

Some villages have a lovely green with, maybe, an "ancient
    oak",
There's usually a seat there, occupied by "ancient folk",
It's there we sit and sun ourselves, surveying what goes on,
And reminisce about the happy times which are now
    long gone.

Of course, there is the Post Office, where we meet on
    'pension days'
And listen to the gossip of people's wayward ways,
The postmistress dare not mention what happened to
    Mrs. Hughes
But within an hour of opening the village knows the news.

Often a village is lucky and has a lovely hall,
It's used by all the meeting groups and hired out to one
    and all,
The W.I. has speakers and puts the Parish Council right
And the Youth Club on a Friday blasts 'music' to the night.

There you'll find a Parish Church where folk meet on a
    Sunday
And the 'Cat and Fiddle' public house,(where they might
    do food one day),
It's good to have a meeting place where people really
    matter,
For you cannot beat a village where they have a good
    old natter.

Who Said There'd be no Harvest?

In March it was very cold
We even had some snow,
Then April added inches of rain
And the cold made our faces glow.

May and June weren't much better,
The farmers were having a fit,
The weather had never been so bad,
It would be the worst harvest yet.

Then in July the sun came out,
The ground became dry with no rain,
Warmth and long days were a boon,
Crops sprung to life again.

Strawberries were in abundance,
Followed by raspberries fine,
Apples and pears, barley and wheat
Vegetables ready in time.

Now Autumn is here again
And the harvest is all gathered in,
God knows what He is doing
So why do we get in a spin?

Bygones

Buses

I wonder if it is still there - Victoria Coaching Station,
The starting point for coaches taking us on vacation,
Coaches red or yellow, coaches blue or green,
Destinations everywhere on boards were clearly seen.

A holiday on the South coast - Eastbourne possibly
Would mean you looked for 'Southdown' to journey to
    the sea,
Or if you preferred the "Kiss me quick" of Margate down
    in Kent,
The maroon and cream of 'East Kent' coach was the one
you must frequent.

Thanet might be a bit too far so to Chatham you could go,
The double decker bus of 'Maidstone and District' was
    there on show,
It might be the 'Green Line' or 'Royal Blue' you'd use,
The choice was very widespread, it was a job to choose.

Of course it maybe that you went north, Scarborough
    was good,
The ' Yorkshire Traction' was your coach which could go
    on to Fleetwood,
There was a ' Leyland', 'Guy', or 'Bristol', 'Dennis', 'Crossley'
    or 'Bedford' engine,
All fitted with 'Plaxton' coachwork to take you for a spin.

Cars

Have you seen the car parks located in each town
Full of mechanical marvels with some jewels in the crown ?
But where are all the best ones, those built with love
    and care,
The sort you would preserve and pass on to your heir ?

The police just loved the Wolseley which served them
    very well
Fitted with a 'Police' sign and glorious ringing bell,
Humber and Lanchester were driven so sedately,
Pity they're not still around instead of tin boxes I've
    seen lately.

I loved my Flying Standard 8 with the flag upon the
    bonnet,
Leather seats and drop - down roof - oh, I could write
    a sonnet,
Riley and Sunbeam Talbot, now these two had some class,
Other makers soon got jealous and put them out to grass.

There was the Allard and the Alvis, I could go on for ever
But it's what they call 'progress' that gets me in a blether,
Cars are made in many countries it seems, our thirst
    to slake,
Just look around the showrooms and you'll find no
    English make.

Comics

I don't want Captain Marvel,
Superman's not bad,
Batman and Robin are 'old hat',
Modern comics make me mad.

Tiger Tims and Chicks Own
Old fashioned they may be,
But little children loved them
And they were good enough for me.

Radio Fun and Film Fun
Were funny and well drawn,
We laughed at all the antics
Their loss we often mourn.

Our Ernie was the character
On Knockouts title page,
Ok, perhaps not relevant now
But greatly loved in its age.

Now they've got rid of Dandy,
Beano's lost Eggo the Ostrich too,
Hotspur, Champion and Rover's gone,
There's nothing now to do.

Fags

What went on behind the bike shed
Stunted future growth,
We huffed and puffed at cigarettes
To stop it we were loath.

Between us we must have tried them all,
Turf, Woodbines, and Craven 'A',
This latter 'did not affect the throat'
Or so they used to say.

Churchmans No 1 was fine
But much too posh for us,
Player's Weights and Kensitas
Created much less fuss.

The girls preferred Passing Clouds
The boys enjoyed the Trawlers,
Park Drive were the favoured ones
By the team of our footballers.

We did not really smoke these brands
That story's rather shaggy,
We only bought these cigarettes
So we could have 'the faggies'.

Groceries

Look inside the larder and see what's close at hand,
Branded uniform products there, or supermarket brands,
But where are the things we used to buy at the
    corner store
There was 'Monk and Glass's' custard, now one make
    is such a bore.

The first gravy cubes on offer were 'Marmite' make,
of course,
You could be sure of what you bought and were not
    using....er....any other source.
Remember the bright blue tin with the picture of
    the child?
'Cerebos' was a great salt, nothing meek and mild.

Also in the corner shop were things if you felt poorly,
'Carters little liver pills', 'Bile Beans' could cure you surely,
If a headache you should have before aspirin was
    invented,
'Daisy Powders' you would take to stop you being
    tormented.

Everything's the same now, we're stripped of all our
    choice,
And if we ever dare complain no one hears our voice.
Bring back the pills and potions and great makes as
    of yore,
So maybe, only maybe,shopping won't be a chore.

Hardware

The best part of the hardware shop
Was the evocative smell,
Even passing the open door
It's contents you could tell.

Take your own can for paraffin,
Supplied straight from the drum,
This was not near 'England's Glory' matches
Or else there could be some fun.

To save your chimney being swept,
'Imp soot destroyer' was sought,
And if your pet was hungry
'Spratts dog food' would be bought.

The house must always be kept clean
So there was 'Pulvo' for the sink,
'Cardinal Red' for the doorstep,
'Zebo' grate polish made you blink.

In all this glorious melee,
Lawn Mowers also were sold,
Suffolk, Webb and Ransomes,
Which were pushed (so I'm told.)

Add spades , various nails and screws,
Plus the odd Dolly Bag,
The DIY stores of today
Are nothing at all like WE had.

Holidays

What's happened to our holidays
When time had to be well spent,
We now get far too many weeks,
(I blame the government).

One week was all we used to have,
If lucky, maybe two,
We sent off for the brochures
To find out what to do.

If we lived on the eastern side
Hunstanton's a good bet,
'Sunny Hunny' they call it,
(Except when it is wet!)

Down in Kent there's Margate,
Packed beaches and golden sand,
Or if you wanted peace and quiet
Broadstairs was close at hand.

Essex folk chose Clacton,
Or Southend-sur–la-mud ,
Whichever one you seemed to choose
The weather was always good.

There's Blackpool on the northern left,
'Skeggie' on the right,
It maybe not so warm up there
But the sun was always bright.

Now folk all seem to go abroad,
To places I can't spell,
They queue for hours in airports
Complaining 'it's just hell'.

Our seaside towns are close at hand
You can get there very fast,
Maybe one day very soon
We'll all re-visit the past.

Shopping

What's happened to the little shops
Which graced our many High Streets?
Shops where we were served so well
And friends we used to meet.

Maypole Dairies, what a shop
Where they provided seats,
You could sit and watch the world go by
And choose most any treat.

Perks and Elmo, smaller shops,
Maybe not the range,
But smiling staff and courtesy
Plus gossip to exchange.

Then there was that well named store,
The 'Home and Colonial',
Where butter was patted to your order
With the greatest ceremonial.

'International' was one of the bigger boys,
It got far too big for its boots,
And was swallowed up by a supermarket
Who does not give two hoots.

The High Street now is barren,
Finance and Charities are there,
I just wish the small shops could return
To give their customer care.

Soap

Washdays will never be the same
Without trusty well loved brands,
Because when you used the dolly tub
You had to watch your hands.

Omo seems to be no more
All lather and so blue,
A cupful placed into the tub
And it knew what it had to do.

Oxydol and Rinso too
Were used in many homes,
And in the boiling copper
They made a lovely foam.

One thing was essential
When it came to boiling 'whites',
The Reckits Blue Bag was a part
To make them gleaming white.

Teatime

The teapot is in daily use
We know just what it's for,
You put the tea and hot water in
Four minutes later you pour,

But does the tea taste better now
Than it did before?
Where's the Mazawatte
I had in days of yore?

Brooke Bond 'divi' tea has gone.
You cut out all the stamps
And spent them on the groceries,
Or else at holiday camps.

George Payne's London factory
Made tea for upper classes,
It often held tasting days
With little tasting glasses.

Do you remember Lyons 'Blue'?
What about Sainsbury's 'Brown'?
The first brings happy memories
The other a furrowed frown.

Friends would come round for a natter,
Politely called "Afternoon Tea",
We would sit and put the world to rights
As contented as can be.

The Grocer

Do you remember that evocative smell?
All grocers smelt the same,
Was it loose soap or parafin casks
Or something to inflame?

The butter was displayed on marble slabs
Then 'patted' to the requested weight,
A choice of New Zealand, Danish or Dutch
To have what you wanted was great.

Sugar also was sold as you needed
Packed in those strong dark blue bags,
The same sort of bags were used for dried fruit
The contents were shown on a tag.

There were biscuits served straight from square tins
As many or few as you liked,
And if money was short in your household
Broken biscuits were sold at half price.

Of course there was something important
Which is now sadly lacking in there,
The smiling grocer's courtesy
Inviting you to wait on the chair.

Variety

I wonder who thought of the concept,
Workers Playtime was so much fun,
"The day war broke out" by Robb Wilton,
And the show had just begun.

Reg Dixon was 'proper poorly'
Arthur English a typical spiv,
Suzette Tarri and Stainless Stephen
Were funny and yet so plaintive.

Remember the serious comedian
Whose name was a theatre sign?
Nosmo King told funny stories
But finished with a serious rhyme.

Elsie and Doris Waters
The Western Brothers too,
Flotsam and Jetsam, Sandy Powell,
They performed and the time just flew.

And so the list goes on and on,
The air's soggy with nostalgia,
These were all our British acts,
No input from Australia.

Whimsy

A Do(d)gy Tail

You sit down 'cos you're feeling dog tired,
Not Fido's idea for with energy he's fired,
He'll start by looking pathetic, then beg
Scratch, bark, maybe even cock his leg.

You get your onesie and start to moan
There's no one else – you're all alone,
You need your trainers 'cos he's a Lurcher
He'll run you around as he's a searcher.

He meets his friend, a flop eared Basset,
With short legs and an itch he cannot scratch it,
And when you fancy a nice hot-dog
Snuffling up comes a British Bulldog

Fido adores the spotty Dalmation,
But totally ignores the big Alsatian,
Along comes Brucie, now he's a Boxer,
He offers his ball but he's a hoaxer.

Ambling along is a little Dachshund,
With legs so short I'd want a refund,
Fido's best mate is a dog called Daniel,
Who is quite a lively Cocker Spaniel

He has a spat with a lanky Greyhound
And loses the battle on the rebound,
Then Fido has a sudden hunch
And bolts off home to have his lunch.

A Marriage of Convenience

Mr Armitage Shanks was an upright man,
A pillar of society,
Miss Kimberley Clarke resided close by
But she was rather flighty.

Mr Armitage Shanks fell deeply in love
It really befitted him,
Miss Kimberley Clarke was also in love
But hers was paper thin.

Mr Armitage Shanks proposed to her
Just like a little boy,
Miss Kimberley Clarke was flattered
And became just, oh so coy.

On the day of the great wedding
Champers flowed to excess,
Miss Kimberley Clarke was all of a dither
And became quite flushed with success.

Black Shuck

This tale is as true as I stand,
In Norfolk's wonderful land
Black Shuck is a ghostly old dog
What wanders the lane by the bog.

For years that old dog's been around
Leaving great footprints in the ground,
You'll see him on all moonlit nights
His red eyes will give you a fright.

I heard him behind me last week
On a night both windy and bleak,
Dead sober I ran down the loke
'cos believe me to see him's no joke.

Now it is a strange thing to me
That he never seems to run free,
When down there to the pub I roam,
That's only when I'm going home.

Dig

They're digging up the road again,
They've done it all before,
Five times, if memory serves me right
Are they looking for earth's core ?

There are many stories going round
About what they hope to find,
The men that keep on doing it
Well – they don't seem to mind.

I'm going down to ask them,
Maybe they'll tell me why -
It must take ten men a lifetime
To do and not know why.

Of course, it simply crossed my mind
The hole is right outside
The Bear and Nettle public house
Wherein they could reside.

So now I know the answer
It no longer is a puzzle,
The first time that they dug it up
They lost one of their shovels.

Done

When we went on holiday
Dad bought a brand new cap,
Mr. Dunn the salesman
Said, "You will not better that."

The first time Dad put it on
It rained and the dye all run,
He took it back to Mr. Dunn
And told him that he'd been done.

Mr. Dunn was not amused
He didn't think Dad was done,
For Mr. Dunn felt he'd been done
But gave Dad another one.

Every year it was the same,
He was done by Mr. Dunn,
The caps were always imperfect
And fell apart in the summer sun.

Year after year he was done by Dunn,
His neighbours felt the same,
But Mr. Dunn stayed in business
Feeling he'd been done the same.

Now one fine day, Mr. Dunn died,
His clients were sure he would burn,
Old Nick agreed that after what he'd done
Mr. Dunn should be done to a turn.

Gone Before

I knew a little garden
Where lovely flowers grow,
And delicious tasting vegetables
All neatly in a row.

There were onions and radishes
Cauliflowers and beet,
All so appetising,
Hoed up very neat.

He was so very proud of it,
It was his pride and joy,
He'd always grown his vegetables
Since he was a boy.

The lady of the house was not
A vegetable fan
And thought, "I'll get rid of them
As quickly as I can".

I know a little garden
Lovely in sun and shade,
There are no veggies growing now
They're dug in with a spade.

Nelson

(As told to a visitor to the great man's birthplace
– Burnham Thorpe, Norfolk)

Dew yew goo down to Burnham Thorpe
Yew'll fin a gret ol' pub,
That called the "Lord Nelson"
'cos thas wer the ol' bor wos.

His Dad he were the vicar
For a tidy good foo 'ears,
When bor 'ratio were older
Together they 'ad their beers.

They say th' ol' vicarage hed a leak
So Nelson wern't born ther',
But thas a barn jist doon the rud
So with the shep 'h shared.

It's sed 'e lerned 'is sailin'
When in 'is boy'ood prime,
'e tuk a boot at Brancaster
At one and six a toime.

There hint no sea in Burnham Thorpe
So 'e hed to goo awa',
But 'tween 'is gallavanting
'ed cum back her to stay.

Thas wer 'e wanted to be buried
But he wer' famis loike,
So they left 'im up in London
But we still got 'is boike.

PC Santa

Santa Claus was in despair
He had no presents – his sack was bare,
Worldly pressure had now caught up
The little children were out of luck.

The elves had been on strike for days,
Santa could not afford minimum pay,
The workshop was below sixty degrees
(The minimum needed so they would not freeze).

The reindeer too wanted equal rights,
They were all men – not a lady in sight,
Donner and Blitzen, Prancer and Cupid
Said eight men with girls names made them feel stupid.

Rudolph then threw a great big wobbly,
His nose blazed bright red and his horns went knobbly,
He felt his nose was being used to please
So he demanded copyright fees.

With 'equal rights' and 'copyright fees',
'elf and safety' brought him to his knees,
Santa felt lost and totally helpless
All because of political correctness.

He suddenly had a bright idea,
Why shouldn't people have Christmas cheer,
He definitely knew what he must do
So Santaland quit membership of the wretched E.U.

Purr-fection

I suppose I am so lucky
To have a mistress in tow,
We rub along together
Going with the flow.

She feeds me well with tempting treats,
Not always to my taste,
And never fails to have a moan
When they go to waste.

I have my special place indoors
And another in the garden,
With private beds and cushions
There's nothing O so 'common'.

She's really very studious
And says her Morning Prayers,
So I snuggle to her closely
And tell her all MY cares.

When I'm feeling playful,
Beneath the table we play 'footsie',
By the way, I ought to mention
I'm a cat, my name is Tootsie.

The Donkey and the Owl

One day the owl was on a bough
'owling by its nest,
The donkey, he stood underneath
Having a well earned rest.

"What do you want?" the donkey assked
"You seem in so much pain,"
"The little ones have gone", it 'owled
"They'd been allowled out again."

To stop the owl from 'owling
The donkey he just brayed,
"I'll go and get the parson",
So he came and prayed.

It's there the story ended,
The youngsters flew back en-mass,
Said the donkey to the 'owling owl,
"It's you that's a silly ass".

Unaffordable

He's banned, the mighty whacker Webb
We can't afford him , that's for sure,
Alright, he can play cricket - but
Last week the club showed him the door.

The trouble is, he can't see what's wrong
His exploits are just the way he tells it,
Cricket balls aren't cheap – we can't afford him
Because he gives them such a hefty hit.

Last week in one match – I tell no lies
He thumped a ball over the boundary tree,
It landed on a lorry passing by
And ended up beside the deep blue sea.

The next ball landed in the river
Which was flowing at its fastest at that time,
The fielders were not quick enough to catch it
It won't be seen again in our lifetime.

One ball hit a sparrow in an oak tree,
And stuck, of course, in the topmost bough,
The umpires did not appear too happy
And the sparrow had to sit and mop its brow.

That was the first three balls sent down in the over
With three balls in the over still to bowl,
Two went right through the clubhouse windows,
At least the last one killed that pesky mole.

Living Life

A Gizmo Called Memory

The latest gimmick that's about really makes me smile,
Just press a single button, or two, and watch TV in style,
For you can now watch past programmes if you missed
    them first time round,
It seems like science fiction and leaves me quite spell
    bound.

Who wants to look at things now past, best look towards
    the future,
Yet, this is what we do all day as if looking at a picture,
Some little thing, a word perhaps, will set our thoughts
    awhirl,
As we remember times long past, misty memories will
swirl.

The happy times we used to share on holidays or at home,
Sandcastles demolished by the tide, that ghastly garden
    gnome,
The first time we went dancing and I took you for a meal,
Our engagement and our wedding, was it really real?

Of course, the sun, it always shone as it was expected to,
We clearly remember many things we'd often say and do,
We do not need a gizmo or consult books in a library,
God gave us instant recall in His gift we call a memory.

Beauty All Around

The river, sunlight dappled, flows gently on its way,
Whilst from the nearby field comes the scent of new-
    mown hay,
Above our heads the glorious song of skylarks flying high
Where fluffy clouds hang motionless in the bright blue sky.

Nearby a baby in its pram, chuckles with delight,
To see the blackbird family take off for their first flight,
A neighbour in his garden mows the lawn, a traditional
    sound,
And somewhere a few miles away the ocean's in its
    bounds.

These sounds and sights are memories coming down the
    years,
Witnessed with our loved ones in joy and sometimes tears,
The world will go on turning and for us it does not care,
But life will bring back memories just for us to share.

Choices

Would you rather shed tears for one who has gone
or remember to smile as you both did all along?

> Do you close your eyes and be very bereft
> Or open your eyes and see all that she left?

Your heart can break because you can't see her
Or be full of the love with which you both share.

> Do you remember that she is not here
> Or let memory live on to bring you much cheer?

Why turn your back on tomorrow and live just for today
Be happy tomorrow because of yesterday.

> You can cry, close your mind, be empty, live in pain
> But she'd wish you to smile, open your eyes and heart
> and live again.

Versified by Paul Scrivener

Choices

Original version as read at the funeral of
H.M. The Queen Mother

You can shed tears that she has gone
  Or you can smile because she has lived

You can close your eyes and pray she'll come back
  Or you can open your eyes and see all that she left

Your heart can be empty because you can't see her
  Or you can be full of all the love you shared

You can turn your back on tomorrow and live for
yesterday
  Or you can be happy for tomorrow because of
  yesterday

You can remember only that she has gone
  Or you can cherish her memory and let it live on

You can cry and close your mind, be empty and turn your
back
  Or you can do what she would wish; smile, open your
  eyes and your heart ... and go on.

(Anon)

Force Ten to Safe Harbour
An allegory of the journey from diagnosis to peace

Tumbling, rumbling, crashing down, the waves land
    on the shore,
Sometimes I wonder where those droplets have
    been before,
Was it on some coral reef, an island in the sun,
Or drifted down from frozen wastes before the
    Gulf Stream run?

Have they seen the world that lurks beneath the
    ocean's swell,
The mysteries and eeriness of which mankind can't tell?
Where predators both large and sleek lurk beneath
    the waves,
Among the many capsized ships laying in watery graves.

Who can fathom this salty world, the tides which ebb
    and flow,
At the mercy of the prevailing winds which constantly
    on it blow,
Sometimes it causes just a ripple and others a mighty swell,
The violent storms and heavy waves of which seasoned
    sailors tell.

St. Elmo's fire plays round the mast, the sky's as black as ink,
The ship is rocked so violently, we are certain it will sink,
Then daylight comes, the wind has dropped, sunrise is
    held in awe,
The sea is calmer, as if to say, 'I've brought you safe to shore.'

Life's Journey

Almost every other day
Someone asks the question,
"Hello, and how are you today?"
Just asking – or suggestion?

How we feel is not what we say,
"OK" or "Very Well",
But deep within our inmost heart
We feel all is not well.

Our loss makes us feel deserted
Only we will know the pain,
It's our belief we'll never say
"OK" honestly again.

Now just look back to those dark days
Which scarred our very being,
Do you still feel just the same,
Or a much improved well being?

Just as the journey we have done
Has slowly helped our way,
Look forward and the future
Provides a better day.

Memorium at Wells

We stood there by the slipway as the inshore boat
    was launched,
A group of maybe fifteen and memories for all
    were stirred,
Slowly the helmsman steered the craft to stand off
    twenty yards,
And above the lapping of the tide a seagull's cry
    was heard.

In the lifeboat house we'd met the crew who'd left
    their jobs to greet us,
Ordinary men who you could easily pass unheeding
    in the street,
Yet many owe their lives to these and all their forebears
For gale force winds and wild mammoth waves
    they cheat.

They and their coxswain are here to show appreciation
    to we fifteen,
For we've gathered to remember our loved ones no
    longer here,
In whose memory we subscribe what we can to help
    their work,
We volunteer our time and cash, they volunteer time
    and fear.

And so at anchor the crew await to hear a name read from
    the list,
As it is said, so rose petals are scattered on the sea,
The flowing tide takes them away to some unknown
    and distant port,
Just as our loved ones sailed from us and arrived at
    the waiting quay.

Message of the Tree

Life is like a Christmas tree
Once standing tall and trim
Until the woodman cut it down,
Which seemed to be a sin.

So, battered and broken, its glory gone,
It's loaded on a truck,
And placed inside the wood yard
It seemed right out of luck.

But then a lady, passing by,
Said,"That's the one I need",
It was sent to her local Parish Church,
With every possible speed.

The tree was decorated
With lights and coloured things,
It stood so tall and lovely
Its' praise did people sing.

It was now far removed
From its' natural wood,
But full of light and beauty
It became more understood.

Our lives can be much brighter
If we remember yesterday
Then brighten up tomorrow
Because we're loved today.

Providence

The old lady sat on the park bench
Watching the world go by,
Young and old, boys and girls,
Tears of memory in her eye.

She remembered the time, now long ago,
With her feet firmly placed on the ground,
She'd walked down the aisle and married her Ted
And there was not a care to be found.

She felt very lonely, especially today
Her birthday, but nobody cared,
There was no one there to speak her name,
This day was no longer shared.

As she sat in a world of her own,
Her hand was suddenly licked wet,
There at her feet sat a little dog,
Obviously somebody's pet.

It looked at her with wistful eyes,
Its expression just mirrored her own,
There was no collar with address tag attached
Like her, it was all alone.

She tried in vain to find where it belonged,
But nobody wanted to know,
So there it stayed with her in her house,
And their companionship started to show.

So from that day she brightened up,
No longer in a perpetual fog,
Not forgotten or weary, a friend she had found
When God sent her that little dog.

Read All About It!

Read all about it! Read all about it! The world is in a mess,
The country's going all to pot, politicians can't care less,
A reactor has blown up and there are thousands dead
Or, maybe, it's only just a few so we'll report
    elsewhere instead.

Read all about it! Read all about it! A ship has
    gone aground,
Its tanks have all split open and there's oil all around,
The TV shows the pictures, seabirds are in a plight,
Press reports all differ, they seldom get it right.

Read all about it! Read all about it! You can't beat a
    good old war,
Journalists fly over there as if to settle a score,
"We'll send in all our army, the US will help out too",
But by the time they're mobilised there's not much
    there to do.

We really mustn't criticise, they try to do their best,
But who can you believe when they know not East
    from West,
We need a guide that's accurate, that makes it all so real,
There's one, it's called 'The Bible', it tells it how we feel,
So if you're down and weary and want lifting up a bit,
Pick up the truth, then find you can, read ALL about it!

Sunrise/Sunset

The sun will always rise each day
Though sometimes obscured by cloud,
Which means we cannot see its brightness
Except when we're allowed.

After brightening up our days
And giving of its best
Casting red-hued patterns
It sinks into the west.

What memories that daylight brought
Depends on what we did.
Did we make the most of it
Or from it's rays we hid?

And so it is with life my friends,
The world's brightened by our birth,
But with the setting of the sun
We can't remain on earth.

For those who mourn the loss of one
Life can be bleak like rain,
But if we raise eyes heavenward
We can see the sun again.

Two Cathedrals

Two kinds of 'cathedral' grace this land
Both with similar trends,
Both give joy and happiness
And that's where similarity ends.

'Cathedral A' seats a thousand
And is full of expectant folk,
The focal point is light and dance
And the occasional joke.

'Cathedral B' seats hundreds,
But just a few non-expectant folk,
The focal point is stained glass
And a cross which was Jesus Christ's yoke.

Both 'cathedrals' have welcomers,
The stage set by a production team,
One offers bright lights and music,
The other offers only a dream.

'Cathedral A' is a theatre,
Where people go to be cheered,
'Cathedral B' is a local church
Where the name of God is feared.

And yet, both 'cathedrals' are similar,
Both sing with a joyful voice,
Both have a musical director
And a chorus to help us rejoice.

Both have directors to organise,
To ensure what the author intends,
Both have a strict understanding
Of the rules which they cannot bend.

Cont.

Christ's message is one of such joy,
The church ought not to be dull,
People must be able to find God is there
And the worship must always be full.

We could take a lesson from the theatre
And follow God's immaculate scheme,
Put worship in the hands of Him who knows,
For God is our producer supreme.

Undying Love

We enjoyed a glorious springtime
When life was fresh and new,
The world was full of promises,
Promises strong and true.

Then came the summer of sweet content,
We took a slower pace,
The sun just kept on shining
But would it always be the case?

Autumn winds began to blow
Our world began to change,
Familiar things and faces
Had gone, it was so strange.

So winter came, its cold and chill
Set our heart to stone,
Where once we enjoyed the seasons
Now we were all alone.

No matter how distraught we are
We must not keep the frost,
Springtime will come round again
Memories keep the one we lost.

We Buried Him Today

C.S. has died, we buried him today,
The parson in his eulogy said we ought to pray,
There'll never be another like him, our world will
    go to pot,
Most people can do something, but he could do the lot.

When people were in trouble he'd give a helping hand,
The elderly would find comfort from his faithful
    nursing band,
He would help the teachers understand and give them
    his support,
And when 'officialdom' appeared they'd get a
    sharp retort.

He took on the ruling classes, made law makers see sense,
Magistrates and judges would not sit on the fence,
Police officers had the confidence to investigate a crime,
He cut through all the paperwork to give them much
    more time.

Motorists took far less risks and accidents were few,
Doctors could get on with their work as could the
    ambulance crew,
Teenagers were understood, children playing just
    the same,
But C.S. now has passed away, - Common Sense was his
    full name.

What's That Building For?

Turning the corner whilst driving along
I suddenly saw a church tower,
Rising above a line of trees
Surely it was there to empower.

Passing the trees I was in the town centre,
There stood the church in the market square,
Centrally placed for the townsfolk to see
Giving refuge and succour and care.

The small Suffolk town has been there for aeons
And the church was built when the folk really cared,
Children Christened, Confirmed and wed there
Generations laughed, wept and worship was shared.

Do those now hurrying past look up
And see the cross gleaming above open door,
Or just hear the clock that chimes the hour
And the building itself they ignore ?

Epilogue

One day, whilst out for a walk
I came upon a gate,
I had not seen it there before
On this great estate.

A notice was on the side of it,
"In nineteen-thirty eight
This was erected especially
On an important date".

The gate was born the same as me,
What a coincidence,
Like me it looked a bit worn out
There's plenty of evidence.

A sign said "Enter, please close the gate",
That set me quite aback,
Why "close" not "shut" the gate I thought,
Could I not go back?

Through the gate I walked an unknown path
Into a glorious sight,
There were friends and loved-ones waiting,
Bathed in Heavenly light.

Index

Acknowledgements

My sincere thanks go to my publisher Vicky Bodo of Sitting Duck Press who has freely given her time and expertise in publishing all three volumes.

Thanks also to Rev'd Nigel Washington, my mentor, and without whose encouragement these poems would have remained on file in my study.

This volume has been proof read by Linda Little to whom I am extremely grateful.

Friends have sparked off thoughts and I wrote verses just for them which are included, with permission, in this book, so my thanks go to Linda and David Carpenter, Cynthia Pitman, Glenis Greenland, Kate Smith, and the late Delli Fulcher. Some poems have appeared in the *Daily Mail*, RNLI Literature, Westoning and Tingrith Parish Link and the *Poppyland Group* magazine.

To all who have given their support to this project -
THANK YOU.